TWIBEL

A GUIDE TO
LIBEL AND CONTEMPT FOR TWEETERS, FACEBOOKERS AND BLOGGERS

by Paul Chantler
and Paul Hollins

Copyright © 2012 by Paul Chantler & Paul Hollins

All Rights Reserved. No part of this publication may be reproduced in any form or by any means, including scanning, photocopying, or otherwise without prior written permission of the copyright holder.

ISBN 978-1-4716-4984-4
Printed in the United Kingdom

Liability Disclaimer:

This book is not a substitute for seeking personalised professional legal advice. It should be understood that the pages of this book do not purport to offer any kind of legal advice whatsoever whether or not implied.

Laws can and do vary widely between countries and jurisdictions; you should therefore always endeavour to do your own thorough due diligence to ensure full compliance with local governing laws.

The author, publisher, distributor and any other third-party associated with this book will not be held responsible under any circumstances for any action taken in whole or in part in respect of the information contained herein.

By reading this document, you assume all risks associated with using the advice given, with a full understanding that you, solely, are responsible for anything that may occur as a result of putting this information into action in any way, and regardless of your interpretation of the advice. Therefore this book should be considered for use as general entertainment purposes only.

Terms of Use:

You are given a non-transferable, "personal use" license to this product. You cannot distribute it or share it with other individuals. It is for your own personal use only.

All copyrights and trademarks remain the sole right of their respective owner. All stories and examples shown are for illustration purposes only.

Dedication from Paul Chantler

With much love to my mum, Joy Chantler

Dedication from Paul Hollins

*To my family and friends
whose support has never ceased to amaze me.*

Contents

Preface xi

Introduction xiii

Part 1: DEFAMATION – Protecting Reputations

What Is Defamation? 3

What Is Libel? 5

What Has To Be Proved? 7

How Does Libel Affect Twitter, Facebook and Blogs? 9

Online Defamation Cases Double 11

Why 'Comedy' Is No Defence 13

Repeating a Libel Is Just as Bad 15

Bloggers Beware! 17

Beware Anonymous Posts 19

Celebs Are Fair Game Though, Right? 21

Beyond Celebrity 23

The Burden of Proof Lies With You 25

If You Can't Prove It –Don't Post It! 27

"Allegedly" Won't Protect You 29

Is Honest Comment a Defence? 31
Does Not Naming the Person Make It OK? 33
'Rumours' and 'Wicked Whispers' Are Risky 35
It's All a Matter of Context 37
Defences to Libel 39
Killer Costs – and Saying Sorry 41
Things You Should Avoid Blogging, Posting and Tweeting 43

Part 2: CONTEMPT OF COURT – The Right to a Fair Trial

What Is Contempt of Court? 47
Tweeting From Court 49
The Danger of Breaking Court Orders 51
More Things to Avoid Tweeting or Posting 53
Consequences of Committing Contempt 55
Why Do Newspapers 'Get Away With' Contempt? 57
The Internet and Juries 59
View From the Top 63

Part 3: INJUNCTIONS – Free Speech Versus Privacy

What Is an Injunction and a Super-Injunction? 67
How Does a Super-Injunction Work? 69
Are Tweeters Waging War on Super-Injunctions? 71
Social Media Is Not Beyond the Law 73
Summing Up 75

About the Authors 77

Preface

Both of us have spent lifetimes in the radio industry.

Our first book together was called *Hang the DJ?* — a legal guide for radio presenters.

It became clear when we wrote it that much of the advice and information about libel and contempt would be useful to a wider readership, in particular those regularly posting on Facebook, tweeting on Twitter and writing blogs.

So we came up with *TWIBEL* and hope it'll be a handy, easy-to-understand guide to a complex area of the law which is becoming increasingly relevant.

It's certain that the number of legal action spurred by online social media will increase over the next few years.

We believe this guide will give you the knowledge to keep on the right side of the law.

Paul Chantler and Paul Hollins
April 2012

Introduction

Once upon a time, if you had a opinion of someone or a gripe with them, you could express your view freely to friends in a bar, cafe or the street.

In today's world of social media, there are many more ways you can say what you think. You can update your Facebook status, post a Tweet on Twitter or have a rant on your online blog.

However while getting it off your chest may be therapeutic, it could get you into big trouble with the law.

What appears to be a casual, throwaway remark on Facebook or Twitter can actually have a huge impact. Once something is written and online for all to see, it's there, it's permanent and the damage is done.

Courts tend to view tweets, posts and blogs as publications, not as private conversations — a distinction many users don't appreciate until it's too late.

Unlike the pre-digital days when only newspapers, radio and television had to worry about the law, now EVERYONE can be a publisher — and you need to be aware of the legal implications of what you do.

There's no doubt Twitter and Facebook have narrowed the gap between simply thinking something and publishing it to a global audience.

Writing something online can be defamatory and mean you can be sued for libel. Or you can be in contempt for revealing something the courts have a right to be kept secret.

There are 800 million users of Facebook worldwide, 200 million Twitter users and 156 million public blogs. With so much opinion being posted online by so many people, there are potentially huge legal risks because most Tweeters, Facebookers and bloggers just don't have a clue of the dangers.

And unlike professional journalists, much of what appears online is written by people who don't necessarily check facts in the way media organisations do.

The intention of this book is to give you an easy-to-understand overview of the laws of defamation and contempt, and how it can affect what you do online.

This book isn't about scaremongering or making you worry unnecessarily. It's simply about helping reduce the risk of finding yourself at the centre of very expensive legal action.

It will help you to avoid Twitter Libel — or 'Twibel' as it's become known — as well as other potential legal problems.

We cover defamation and libel as well as contempt of court and privacy, including injunctions.

Please note that the content is based on the legal system of England and Wales, although we use examples from other countries. The detail of libel law differs in other jurisdictions, so please be sure to check.

These days, nothing said online is really private. So be careful what you tweet...

[Part 1]

DEFAMATION
• • •
Protecting Reputations

What Is Defamation?

The word defamation literally means to "de-fame" someone. In other words, harming their reputation.

The law says everyone has a right to a good name throughout their lives, unless there is undeniable evidence to the contrary such as being convicted of a crime.

Defamation is divided into two parts — Slander and Libel.

> SLANDER is spoken defamation. Anyone suing for slander has to prove an actual loss or damage, for example that someone has lost money or their job.

> LIBEL is published defamation in a newspaper, book, magazine, on radio or television — or written on a blog or a social networking site, such as Twitter or Facebook.

People sometimes also sue for MALICIOUS FALSEHOOD. This means a statement is a lie told with malice. In other words, the person making it knew what they were saying was false and would cause harm or damage.

What Is Libel?

This is important to understand as it's the legal definition of libel.

Libel is anything published or broadcast which:-

> Exposes someone to HATRED, RIDICULE, CONTEMPT or DISGRACE.

> Leads someone to be SHUNNED or AVOIDED.

> Injures someone in their BUSINESS, OFFICE, TRADE or PROFESSION.

> LOWERS someone in the eyes of the general public.

What Has To Be Proved?

In order for a libel action to succeed against you, someone ONLY has to prove:

> The statement is defamatory

> The statement refers to them

> The statement was published by you

They DO NOT have to prove:

> The statement is false — the burden of proof is on you.

> The statement did any real damage — it's sufficient that it simply discredits someone

How Does Libel Affect Twitter, Facebook and Blogs?

Libel law protects individuals and organisations from unwarranted, mistaken or untruthful attacks on their reputation and good name.

When you post on a blog or on Twitter or Facebook, you actually have a real responsibility for what you write.

It's important you're aware of your legal obligations because the consequences of getting it wrong can be incredibly severe.

You can end up being sued personally for damages and the legal costs both of which could run into thousands of pounds.

A lack of knowledge is no defence. A casual, throwaway remark can result in legal action against you.

Libel is all about the meaning of words or phrases and what a reasonable person understands and thinks about them.

This covers INFERENCE, IMPLICATION and INNUENDO.

It's worth remembering that it's not just famous people who sue for libel. Anyone can bring legal proceedings if they believe they have a case.

A former mayor of Caerphilly in South Wales made legal history when he became the first person in Britain to pay damages for libel on Twitter.

Colin Elsbury was ordered by the High Court in Cardiff to pay £3,000 compensation after he mistakenly tweeted that political rival Eddie Talbot had to be removed by police from a polling station.

In addition to the payment of damages, Mr Elsbury was also left with a bill for legal costs of about £50,000.

He also had to publish a formal apology on his Twitter feed for damaging Mr Talbot's reputation and for causing him to suffer anger, upset and ridicule.

Online Defamation Cases Double

The number of court cases brought by people who say they've been defamed online more than doubled in 2010/11.

Internet-related libel cases in England and Wales went up from seven to 16 in the year ending 31st May 2011, according to legal information company Sweet and Maxwell.

The increase is being linked to a rise in the use of social media sites like Facebook and Twitter.

One legal firm, Hugh James Solicitors in Cardiff, says it has taken forward six defamation actions involving Facebook recently. Many of the cases involved unfounded allegations.

One case from Hugh James in Cardiff involved a woman who worked with children. An associate of hers posted allegations of violence on her Facebook wall.

The woman's employer and her regulatory body saw the comments and this led to a big investigation.

However the woman was fully acquitted and the case was settled out of court.

The settlement involved retractions and written apologies to every person who was a prospective employer.

Why 'Comedy' Is No Defence

The law does not have a sense of humour.

What you might consider a joke or humorous comment can easily be libellous.

Many TV and radio comedy shows air comments and insults about celebrities and politicians — but it is done within the context of a well established and well known format which ordinary viewers and listeners are unlikely to take seriously.

The same can't necessarily be said about blogs or social media postings. How could the casual reader of a tweet know you're making a joke?

Also TV comedy shows are cleverly edited to give the impression that 'anything goes' and the participants can say whatever they want.

In reality, the content of these shows is screened by a professional team of lawyers ahead of transmission to ensure anything broadcast stays well within acceptable boundaries.

Even if you make clear a comment you make is a joke, it can still get you into trouble.

A highly-experienced presenter on a radio station in the North of England read out an email in 2005 from a listener inquiring about a former DJ who used to be on air some years before.

The presenter named the DJ and said: "He's alright. He's just come out of prison. The kiddy fiddling charges were dropped." He laughed as he quickly added; "only joking of course!"

The radio station was sued for libel by the person referred to — and had to pay damages of several thousand pounds and broadcast an apology.

Repeating a Libel Is Just as Bad

Did you know that simply repeating a libel on your blog or social media feed is enough for someone to take legal action against you?

In the eyes of the law, it doesn't matter if you're quoting from another source; if you repeat a libel you are as much to blame for publishing it as the original source.

Always be VERY CAREFUL when using a newspaper or magazine story as the basis of a blog or tweet.

You should also exercise EXTREME CARE when researching stories on the internet. Some sites are most trustworthy than others, for example the BBC website.

But be careful when using sites like Wikipedia which can be amended by users.

Many people — celebrities in particular — have taken legal action over stories that were found to be untrue.

Bloggers Beware!

Bloggers think that free speech allows them to write — and encourage others to write — what they like.

They can't. The law of libel applies to them and their contributors too.

Bloggers have to be particularly careful if they allow comments on their blogs.

Comments can be administered in two ways on blogs — firstly, "We never moderate — all comments go up automatically", and secondly, "All comments are read and manually approved".

The latter approach gives a better quality of comment but can also bring a potential legal danger.

If a comment has been reviewed and published by the blogger and the comment is subsequently found to be libellous, it is the BLOGGER who's responsible and not the original author of the comment.

The blogger has simply repeated a libel.

Beware Anonymous Posts...

If a blog or website fails to take down a user's anonymous defamatory post after receiving a complaint, they risk being treated as the primary publisher and sued for libel.

One proposal by a parliamentary committee for libel reform is that blogs and websites should have libel protection if they act quickly to remove anonymous postings which prompt a complaint.

It says blogs which identify authors of comments and publish complaints alongside should get protection too. But this is not law yet.

The committee says the aim is to reduce damage "inflicted by the mischievous and the malicious".

But organisations like the parenting website Mumsnet argue that many of its members rely on the ability to make comments under a user name.

They acknowledge the right to stop people from "assassinating the character of others from behind the cloak of anonymity" but say the proposals could stifle honesty about difficult real-life situations and lead to more demands for posts to be removed.

The parenting website Mumsnet.com settled a libel case in 2007 over comments posted on its website by users.

Baby expert Gina Ford, author of the book *Contented Little Babies*, launched libel action after allegedly insulting comments about her appeared on the site's discussion boards.

One comment is said to have compared her to a Middle East terrorist.

The case was settled out of court with payment of compensation and costs as well as the publication of an apology on the website.

Celebs Are Fair Game Though, Right?

WRONG! It's a mistake to think that just because someone chooses to be in the public eye that they're 'fair game' and that you can therefore say anything you like about them.

There are numerous examples of libel payouts when inaccurate stories about celebrities and their private lives have been splashed over the pages of a newspaper.

However, sometimes celebrities themselves can be vulnerable to legal action — especially in these days when they have unfettered access to their own mouthpieces in the form of a Twitter feed.

US singer Courtney Love paid more than £260,000 ($430,000) in 2011 to settle the world's first Twitter Libel — or 'Twibel' — lawsuit.

She agreed an out-of-court settlement with her fashion designer Dawn Simorangkir rather than risk going to trial over what legal papers described as a string of defamatory comments in tweets on her former Twitter account courtneylover79.

Among other things, Miss Simorangkir was accused of being "a nasty, lying hosebag thief".

Miss Love, the widow of Nirvana frontman Kurt Cobain, argued that her rantings were merely an opinion and that Miss Simorangkir couldn't prove how they damaged her.

But the designer claimed Miss Love was influential as an entertainer and noted the power of social media to disseminate damaging comments.

Even though the case didn't go to trial, it's set a disturbing precedent in the US where freedom of speech generally trumps accusations of libel.

Beyond Celebrity

Social media related libel litigation extends beyond the scope of celebrities and individuals. Here are two examples of how libel has been used in commercial cases involving companies:-

---

Pizza Kitchen, a U.S. pizza restaurant, was sued for libel in 2009 for posting various tweets accusing a marketing firm, Low and Tritt, of being crooks and thieves.

As a result of the tweets, Low and Tritt filed a $2 million libel suit against Pizza Kitchen.

Chicago property company, Horizon Group Management, filed a libel suit in 2009 against a tenant who complained about her "mouldy apartment" on Twitter.

The company claimed the tenant "maliciously and wrongfully published the false and defamatory tweet."

The case was dismissed on a technicality as the judge felt the tweet was too vague to meet test of libel; the tenant had not specifically referred to the company in Chicago but had simply mentioned "Horizon Realty".

The Burden of Proof Lies With You

Almost uniquely in English law, the burden of proof in libel cases lies with the writer and publisher, NOT the complainant.

In other words, YOU have to be able to prove that what you write on your blog or social media page is true. The person you've targeted doesn't have to prove that you're wrong or any statement about them is false.

This is a key distinction; it's important you understand this.

For example, if you described someone in a tweet as a "junkie" and they took action against you, it's up to you to prove in court that they have a drug problem.

One of the most effective ways to protect yourself against the threat of libel is to use only verifiable facts. A verifiable fact is one that is capable of being proven true or false.

So, ask yourself: Is this true? Can I prove it? Would I like this said about me?

If You Can't Prove It – Don't Post It!

One of the most important points is to make absolutely sure that what you write on Twitter, Facebook and your blog is 100% true.

Do NOT make claims or accusations that you cannot prove in court.

Even if you think you can prove it, still be very cautious as proving things in court can be very difficult indeed.

You'll have to use robust documentary evidence or first-hand corroboration from one or more people willing to testify in court.

Therefore, it's essential you make sure you get your facts right before you say what you think of an individual or organisation online.

"Allegedly" Won't Protect You

Comedians Paul Merton and Ian Hislop have a lot to answer for when it comes to libel.

Their use of the word "allegedly" over the years on the satirical TV quiz *Have I Got News For You* became a running joke — and has lulled people into believing that if they used it too, they can say what they like about anyone.

Nothing could be further from the truth.

In fact, using the word allegedly before a potentially dodgy remark about some gives the clear impression you REALISE what you're about to say is dangerous.

It's perceived as admittance that you're not sure whether what you're saying is true.

Have I Got News For You is the perfect example of why TV and radio comedy shows get away with not being sued for libel.

If things are presented in a light-hearted or satirical way on a comedy show, there's far less chance of being sued than if allegations are on a news bulletin.

The key is that people must be aware of the type of show.

Merton and Hislop have built a reputation for comedy and satire over the years — and they also have a team of lawyers who sit through the recording and editing process!

Is Honest Comment a Defence?

YES. The law allows people to have honestly-held opinions.

An honestly held opinion is not libellous in itself — as long as the opinion is not malicious, derogatory or could cause harm to someone's reputation.

That's why we can criticise performers, politicians, footballers and celebrities.

And opinion must actually be comment and not fact.

For example if you attended a concert by a band and you thought the lead-singer's vocal performance was "rubbish", that's fine because it's your honestly held opinion.

However, if you also added "it was so bad people were walking out" then you could be sued unless you can prove in court that people were indeed walking out.

Remember it's up to you to prove it — not for the singer (or anyone else) to deny it.

The reason you could have action taken against you is that by adding the statement that "people were walking out," it may negatively influence someone else's opinion of the band.

It could even cause financial harm to them if that person decides to seek a refund on their ticket rather than see them in concert.

You can criticise someone's performance — but to imply they weren't trying could be libellous.

You can't go over-the-top with criticism either.

The actress Charlotte Cornwall sued tabloid newspaper the Sunday People and its columnist Nina Myskow in 1985 for commenting about a theatre performance in her 'Wally of the Week' column: "She can't sing, her bum is too big and she has the sort of stage presence that jams lavatories."

She was awarded £11,000 damages because the judge said that criticism must not "pass out of the domain of criticism itself." In other words, critics can't make derogatory statements in the guise of criticism.

Does Not Naming the Person Make It OK?

NO. Again, this is a popular misconception. The law states that if the person is simply identifiable then they can take legal action.

The word 'identifiable' is key as it means that even if you don't directly name the person, they can still launch legal proceedings against you if people can work out who they are from what you said or the way you described them.

If a person or group can establish that the offending words apply to them, they have a case.

And remember, you can libel companies and organisations as well as individuals.

It's difficult for action to be taken in the case of wide generalisations but not as things get more specific.

For example, "All estate agents are liars and cheats" is unlikely to be actionable. But if you say, "All estate agents in Blanktown High Street are liars and cheats", they're identifiable and could all take you to court.

'Rumours' and 'Wicked Whispers' Are Risky

A comment can still be libellous even if it is reported as a rumour.

Worse still, it can also be libellous even if you acknowledge it as being untrue.

For example, if you were to post or tweet something like, "There's a rumour going around that Frank at the corner-shop has been selling out-of-date food, but don't worry because the stuff I've bought there has always been fine" it could still be considered libellous.

This is because the 'rumour part' is based on a defamatory comment which you are effectively repeating.

Therefore if Frank believes that because you mentioned this rumour exists and you are perpetuating it, he could claim that you are further damaging his name, reputation and trade; and as a result could take action against you.

Remember — If he were to do so, he is under no obligation to prove that he HASN'T been selling out of date food but you may to have prove in court that he was because you repeated the libellous rumour.

Always take great care with how you approach rumours, so you don't put yourself at risk.

It's All a Matter of Context

There are times where you need to exercise a greater level of care to avoid libel when commenting online or describing a person.

For example, it's fine to describe someone as "all fingers and thumbs" in everyday life.

However if you were using that phrase to describe a prominent neurosurgeon, then it could be deemed libellous. This is because the description you have used is derogatory.

A neurosurgeon naturally needs a steady hand, so being described as "all fingers and thumbs" leads to a negative perception.

This could easily damage his reputation and therefore cause harm professionally.

The area of context is one where you need to take great care. Even if what you're posting or tweeting is intended to be funny, the impact of your words could put you on the wrong side of law.

Defences to Libel

There are three main defences to libel:

> **Justification** — The matter is true both in substance and in fact. Remember, though, the burden of proof is on you. If the substance is sufficiently true, a court may overlook minor details of fact.

> **Honest Comment** — If the remarks are statements of opinion rather than fact, then it's an acceptable defence to say that the comment was made in good faith, without malice and on a matter of public concern.

> **Privilege** — This is a complex legal defence based on public interest, which applies to parliament and court hearings. Absolute Privilege covers what MPs say in Parliament and what people (witnesses, lawyers, judges) say in court. Qualified Privilege protects accurate and fair reports of those proceedings by newspapers, radio and television.

It's worth noting that you can't libel people who are dead.

Killer Costs – and Saying Sorry

Libel is a CIVIL rather than a criminal matter. This means matters are settled by the payment of damages and offer of apologies rather than a prison sentence.

If you're sued for libel, the legal fees and payment of damages can run into thousands of pounds.

Newspapers, radio and television stations have defamation insurance which covers the cost of damages and legal fees.

If you tweet, post or blog regularly, it might be worth considering the purchase of Professional Indemnity Insurance which would cover you in the unfortunate event of legal action being taken against you.

Choose a reputable insurer and enquire about taking out a policy.

The other cost to consider, apart from the ones above, is that of personal impact. Being the subject of legal action puts huge pressure on an individual, financially, emotionally and professionally.

In addition to damages and costs, the settlement of a libel action usually requires an apology either read out in court or, from time to time, posted online.

Apologies need careful wording so leave this to the lawyers and don't try to say sorry yourself without advice as it could get you into even more trouble.

In Malaysia, a political activist agreed to apologise multiple times on Twitter in an unusual settlement of a libel case.

Fahmi Fadzil agreed he had defamed a magazine called *Female* and a publishing company, BluInc Media.

As part of the settlement, he retracted what he'd said and sent a tweet apologising 100 times over three days to make amends.

Things You Should Avoid Blogging, Posting and Tweeting

You should always exercise care before writing on Facebook, Twitter or on your blog.

These are the types of things you should avoid, to help ensure you don't find yourself in legal trouble with libel.

> Accusing people of crimes they have not committed

> Alleging they are incompetent

> Alleging they are a hypocrite

> Alleging they are obnoxious

> Alleging they are negligent

> Alleging they are dishonest or immoral

> Accusing them of sexual or financial impropriety

> Accusing them of lying

> Accusing them of doing disreputable deeds

Danger Words...

The following is a list of 'Danger Words' — words you should be very cautious about using.

All these words are potentially libellous.

This list is by no means exhaustive but it will give you a good idea of the types of words you should always strive to avoid:

adulterous	hypocrite	rapist
bankrupt	immoral	retarded
bribery	incompetent	rip-off
compulsive liar	insane	satanic
communist	insolvent	scab
con	junkie	shyster
corrupt	liar	sleazebag
coward	mafia	slut
criminal	mentally diseased	snitch
crook	misappropriated funds	spy
drug addict	Nazi	stupid
drug dealer	odd-ball	swindling
evil	paranoid	thieving
fake	pervert	traitorous
fraud	pimp	unethical
fascist	plagiarist	unprofessional
gold-digger	prostitute	unscrupulous
like Hitler	queer	unsound
homosexual	racist	vile

[Part 2]

CONTEMPT OF COURT

...

The Right to a Fair Trial

What Is Contempt of Court?

Contempt of Court is about protecting people's right to a fair trial. It is separate to libel but equally as important.

One of the main ways you can commit contempt is to influence the jury in a trial by commenting on an ongoing court case.

Legal proceedings start from the moment anyone is arrested or charged.

You become guilty of contempt when you post, tweet or blog material that PREJUDICES or IMPEDES a trial.

The main test for contempt is whether something has created a SUBSTANTIAL RISK of SERIOUS PREJUDICE to active legal proceedings.

It doesn't matter whether you intended to commit contempt; the law presumes you did.

Your opinion (based on what you may have read in the newspapers, seen on TV or heard on the radio) could easily colour the view of a juror reading comments on Twitter, Facebook or a blog.

Tweeting From Court

Video and audio recording has long been barred from courts. In general that applies to tweeting and texting too.

Members of the public are NOT allowed to tweet or text from court without permission.

The Lord Chief Justice, Lord Judge, says the danger of tweeting is likely to be most acute during criminal trials.

"Witnesses who are out of court may be informed of what has already happened in court and so coached or briefed before they then give evidence," he said in guidance issued in December 2011.

In addition, ordinary people in the public gallery could hear information that the jury may have been prevented from hearing, for example the identity of a rape victim. But this cannot be reported.

Therefore the danger of a trial being seriously prejudiced or impeded is obvious.

However, the guidance says bona fide journalists ARE allowed to tweet without permission because they understand the rules and don't pose a danger of interference to the proper administration of justice.

"Twitter as much as you wish," he told journalists as he delivered the guidance, which covers the use of electronic devices including mobile phones and small handheld laptops for live text-based communications.

Explaining why journalists should be treated differently from the public, Lord Judge said: "The difference is that John and Jane Citizen are less likely to understand the rules of contempt than most journalists who come into my court."

The Danger of Breaking Court Orders

Although commenting on a case is one way you can commit contempt, there are various other ways.

> Revealing previous convictions before the end of a trial

> Naming rape victims

> Identifying child witnesses

> Naming blackmail victims

> Publicising details of people in a witness protection programme

Usually all these things are covered by court orders which must not be breached.

Everyone is a reporter these days. Some journalists and lawyers are worried that Tweeters, Facebookers and bloggers will fail to understand the impact of breaking court orders.

More Things to Avoid Tweeting or Posting

> Saying someone has confessed or admitted the crime when they haven't

> Accusing somebody of a more serious crime

> Revealing prosecution evidence before the trial gets underway

> Making derogatory comments suggesting a motive

> Failing to say whether the defendant denies the charges

> Saying whether you believe someone is innocent or guilty

> Seeking or revealing jury deliberations

Consequences of Committing Contempt

Unlike libel which is a CIVIL matter and settled with the award of damages and apologies, contempt of court is a CRIMINAL matter.

This means it carries serious penalties and punishments. You could actually be imprisoned for something you write online.

If you commit contempt, a judge can issue a summons for you to appear in court and you can be arrested.

A contempt case is usually only closed once you have "purged your contempt", in other words sincerely apologised in open court before a judge.

In serious cases, being found guilty of contempt can lead to an unlimited fine and up to two years in prison.

The best advice here is — NEVER EVER discuss or comment on an ongoing trial or pending court case.

You should also ensure you don't comment on someone after they've been arrested or a warrant has been issued for their arrest.

And the consequences of committing contempt don't just end with you. There are much bigger considerations.

For example, your tweets and posts could prejudice a trial and lead to a guilty person walking free. Or a re-trial might have to be arranged at a potential cost of thousands of pounds.

Unguarded tweets, posts and blogs could put the life of a protected witness in danger or cause serious psychological damage to the victim of sexual assault.

Court reporting is a specialized journalistic skill and should be left to the professionals.

The crime editor of The Times newspaper, Sean O'Neill, who tweets regularly under the name TimesCrime, says Twitter can be very useful for journalists.

However, he adds: "Nowadays every Tom, Dick and Harry thinks they can tweet from court."

He says on many occasions, so-called citizen journalists simply don't know what they're doing.

Two presenters at radio station Rock FM in Preston, Mark Kaye and Judith Vause, were arrested and taken to court for something they said on air during the trial of Dr Harold Shipman in 2000.

They commented on the length of the trial and how they thought Dr Shipman was guilty.

The incident was considered so serious because jurors might have heard what the presenters said on their way home from the trial (which was taking place at Preston Crown Court), thus potentially prejudicing the case.

It could have led to the abandonment of the trial costing taxpayers hundreds of thousands of pounds.

Luckily, none of the jurors had heard the broadcast.

The radio station boss had to "purge the contempt" by sincerely apologising to the court and the judge.

Why Do Newspapers 'Get Away With' Contempt?

Many people question why tabloid newspapers avoid prosecution for ignoring the law by publishing details after someone has been arrested.

They rely on a defence known as the 'fade factor', that is the gap between publication and trial which can often be up to 10 months.

The longer the gap, the less the "substantial risk of serious prejudice" of the jury.

However when someone is arrested and subsequently released after questioning without charge, newspapers can find themselves not only at risk of prosecution for contempt but also at risk of libel action.

Chris Jefferies, a 65-year-old retired schoolteacher, was arrested after the murder in Bristol of Jo Yeates in 2010.

Immediately after his arrest, tabloid newspapers described him variously as "strange", "weird", "lewd", "creepy", a stalker, a peeping tom and linked him to previous paedophile and murder cases.

He was released after questioning and never charged. Another man was convicted.

Not only did Mr Jefferies accept substantial libel damages and apologies from eight newspapers but two of them were also successfully prosecuted for Contempt of Court and fined £18,000 and £50,000.

Giving evidence to the Leveson Inquiry into Press Ethics in December 2011, Mr Jefferies said: "In the coverage of my case, there was flagrant lawlessness. The smears were so extensive that it's true to say there will always be people who don't know me who will retain the impression that I'm some kind of very weird character indeed who is best avoided."

The Internet and Juries

If you're selected to be on a jury at a trial, the judge will warn you against researching the history and background online as well as tweeting, posting and blogging about the case.

This is because juries are meant to make up their mind only from the evidence that is presented in court and not be influenced by other things.

Research published in 2010 showed that, for the first time, jurors were going to the internet to look for background to cases. In standard trials, 5% of jurors admitted doing this. In high profile trials, the number was nearly three times this.

It may be that the principle of the sanctity of the jury room cannot be maintained in the face of modern communications and social media.

Of course, jury members have always been able to go to a library to look things up, be influenced by friends and gossip with neighbours. It's just that the internet and social media makes it simpler and easier.

It's important that the integrity of the jury system should be preserved and protected.

When you serve on a jury, you take an oath. When you disobey that oath or when you disobey the orders of a judge — and you're found out — you are likely to be held in contempt of court.

The Lord Chief Justice, Lord Judge, says a custodial sentence for a juror doing this is "virtually inevitable"

A juror who contacted a defendant via Facebook, causing a £6 million drugs trial to collapse, was jailed for eight months for contempt of court.

Joanne Fraill, 40, of Blackley, Greater Manchester, admitted contacting Jamie Sewart, 34, who had already been cleared in the drugs case.

Sewart was also found guilty of contempt and given a two-month suspended sentence for two years.

Fraill admitted making Facebook contact with Sewart and discussing the case while the jury's deliberations were still continuing.

The High Court heard Fraill tracked down Sewart on Facebook and sent her an initial message saying, "You should know me — I've cried with you enough".

Courts are finding it difficult to ensure jurors do not use the internet to investigate cases they are trying in an era when looking up things on a computer seems an increasingly natural instinct.

A juror who used the internet to research a criminal defendant's past was jailed for six months.

Theodora Dallas, 34, a psychology lecturer at the University of Bedfordshire, was found guilty of contempt of court in January 2012 by three High Court judges.

Dallas, who conducted her research at home, was a juror in a trial at Luton Crown Court of a man accused of causing grievous bodily harm.

The judge had to halt the case after discovering what had happened.

The Lord Chief Justice, Lord Judge, says: "Misuse of the internet by a juror is always the most serious irregularity and an effective custodial sentence is almost inevitable."

The Supreme Court in the U.S. state of Arkansas threw out a death row inmate's murder conviction because a juror tweeted during court proceedings.

Erickson Dimas-Martinez appealed against his 2010 murder conviction because a juror used Twitter despite the judge's specific instruction not to communicate with anyone about the case.

The juror, Randy Franco, wrote in one tweet: "Choices to be made. Hearts to be broken... we each define the great line."

Less than an hour before the jury announced its verdict, Franco tweeted: "It's over".

Dimas-Martinez was sent to death row for robbing and shooting a teenager after a party.

View From the Top

The Government's chief law officer, the Attorney General, made an important speech about defamation and contempt at City University's school of journalism in London in December 2011.

Dominic Grieve made it clear that bloggers and tweeters should not consider themselves immune from the law.

He said the revolution in communication methods cannot change essential principles: "The internet does not provide some form of immunity from prosecution."

Mr Grieve went on: "Unlike major news organizations, which on the whole act in a responsible and measured manner, the inhabitants of the internet often feel themselves to be unconstrained by the laws of the land.

"There is a certain belief that so long as something is published in cyberspace, there is no need to respect the laws of contempt or libel. This is mistaken.

"Whilst I accept the danger posed to the administration of justice by many bloggers is minimal, we should not underestimate the potential for a blog or tweet to go viral."

[Part 3]

INJUNCTIONS
...
Free Speech Versus Privacy

What Is an Injunction and a Super-Injunction?

An INJUNCTION is a court order which prevents the publication of certain details of a legal case including identities or actions.

Injunctions — sometimes known as 'gagging orders' — were originally created to protect people whose lives might be at risk if their details were made public, such as child sex offenders.

However, with the passing of the Human Rights Act 1998, judges began to extend the powers of injunctions. Entertainers, sports stars, actors and many more have used injunctions to protect their privacy.

A SUPER-INJUNCTION is a powerful legal order which not only prevents the media from reporting the details of a story covered by an injunction, but also forbids mention of the very existence of the injunction itself.

Users ignoring injunctions or reporting the existence of super-injunctions could be found guilty of contempt of court and sued for invasion of privacy, while those making false accusations could be sued for libel.

How Does a Super-Injunction Work?

The best way to see how an super-injunction works is to examine a hypothetical example.

A Premiership football star asks the High Court to stop a Sunday newspaper publishing a kiss-and-tell story, saying he's a victim of blackmail by a girl he met at a party.

If a judge agrees to a super-injunction, the newspaper is not only stopped from reporting the allegations but is also prevented from saying that the footballer went to court to gag the paper.

If the newspaper breaks this super-injunction by reporting the existence of an injunction, the editor could be prosecuted for being in contempt of court.

It's said super-injunctions are very rarely granted and only for short periods.

More common is an ANONYMISED INJUNCTION where not only is something legally stopped but the names of either or both parties to the proceedings are not revealed.

Are Tweeters Waging War on Super-Injunctions?

Twitter has found itself at the centre of the debate about super-injunctions.

While newspapers, broadcasters and other traditional mainstream media are being restricted in what they can report, thousands of Twitter users have posted tweets and re-tweets circulating information covered by injunctions and super-injunctions.

Are these tweeters beyond the reach of the law?

In practice, legal experts expect tweeters to find safety in numbers if enough defy an injunction simultaneously.

It's not the letter of the law that protects tweeters, but the sheer difficulty of singling out and tracking down so many offenders.

Legal analyst Joshua Rozenberg says: "Clearly they are at risk, but if there are a lot of them there's little chance of them being prosecuted... although if there was one individual who could be seen to have instigated the whole thing, that would be very different."

Footballer Ryan Giggs obtained an injunction to prevent publication of details of an alleged affair with reality TV star Imogen Thomas.

Newspapers and broadcasters were initially unable to name Giggs or even refer to the existence of an injunction.

However on 8th May 2011, a tweeter revealed Giggs' identity. Public interest was such that the record for visits to Twitter was exceeded.

The allegations were repeatedly retweeted by many users making it difficult to prosecute any one individual.

Neverthelesss, legal action was instigated by Giggs against Twitter in an attempt to obtain information on which tweeters were involved.

Paradoxically, this then led to the footballer's name and the allegations being repeated many more times across the internet and, as a consequence, by the mainstream media.

Many newspaper editorials then decried the way injunctions limited free speech and the way they instigated a privacy 'law' by judicial precedent.

Social Media Is Not Beyond the Law

When details of injunctions and super-injunctions began featuring on Twitter, it was assumed the war of the web had been won.

New online platforms didn't obey the same rules as traditional media and it was pointless for courts, governments or regulators to try to intervene.

Technology gives people the ability to band together and challenge authority in ways that were unimaginable a few years ago.

But now things look different and the final outcome remains unclear.

It seems that Twitter is keen to uphold its constitutional first amendment rights to free speech — but, as an American company, is less eager to defy the courts.

When a court in California orders the company to reveal details of a British account holder in a defamation case, it appears the policy is that Twitter first informs him or her and then does as it's told.

And what will happen in the future?

The Lord Chief Justice, Lord Judge, is on record as saying that ways will be found "similar to those used against child pornography" to prevent what he described as the misuse of modern technology.

He said: "Are we really going to say that somebody who has a true claim for privacy, perfectly well made, which the newspapers and media can't report, has to be at the mercy of somebody using modern technology?

"At the moment that may seem to be the case, but I'm not giving up on the possibility that people who in effect peddle lies about others may one day be brought under control, maybe through damages."

Summing Up...

Twitter, Facebook and blogs can create a storm in a matter of minutes, sometimes without a story even having a hint of truth.

For example, tweets have been posted announcing the death of countless celebrities still very much alive.

Social media also has the capacity for providing an easy emotional outlet for individuals to vent about daily worries and perceived insults.

However, you MUST be careful what you write as there's an ever-looming possibility of causing serious harm with ill-judged emotionally-based vitriol.

While you may be in the privacy of your own home or office, posting on a blog or social media site is a public act and should be treated as such.

Once a tweet has been posted, it can't be recalled and there could be serious consequences regardless of the fact that the message is only 140 characters

What was once tittle-tattle is now online forever. Put another way, your words CAN and WILL come back to haunt you.

Eventually legal conventions and social rules may acknowledge that an angry tweet or post is likely to be considered less defamatory than a published article.

But we're not there yet.

Remember:

Tweet in haste,

Repent at leisure.

The best advice:

If in doubt, leave it out.

About the Authors

PAUL CHANTLER has spent 25 years in the industry as a journalist, presenter, producer and programme executive. He was Group Programme Director at three of the UK's biggest radio groups in the 1990s and over the last ten years has built a highly successful international radio consultancy company with clients in the UK, Ireland, Europe and India. He is co-author of the book *Essential Radio Journalism*, originally published 20 years ago.

You can contact Paul Chantler at United Radio
paul.chantler@unitedradio.co.uk
www.unitedradio.com

PAUL HOLLINS is a radio presenter who has been on-air in most of the major markets in the UK. He started his career at Key 103 Manchester before working at BRMB in Birmingham, Capital FM London and London's Heart 106.2. In 1999 he set-up the radio content and syndication company Blue Revolution which is now one of Europe's largest providers of programming and radio services.

You can contact Paul Hollins at Blue Revolution
paul@bluerevolution.com
www.bluerevolution.com

www.ingramcontent.com/pod-product-compliance
Lightning Source LLC
Chambersburg PA
CBHW030915180526
45163CB00004B/1841